# Changing Communities

by Ellen Bari

Editorial Offices: Glenview, Illinois • Parsippany, New Jersey • New York, New York
Sales Offices: Needham, Massachusetts • Duluth, Georgia • Glenview, Illinois
Coppell, Texas • Ontario, California • Mesa, Arizona

# Long Ago

Long ago, many houses in the United States were made of wood. Some houses were smaller than those built today. Heat in a house usually came from a fire in a fireplace.

Over the years **communities** have changed. A community is a group of people. A **neighborhood** is where people live, work, and play.

# Today

Today, wood is still used to build houses. Concrete, bricks, glass, and steel are also used. It takes lots of things to build a house.

Many homes in the United States now have heat, running water, and **electricity**. Electricity is a form of energy.

# Long Ago

Long ago, many people wrote letters by hand using pen and paper. They sent these letters to family and friends who lived far away. It could take a long time for the letters to arrive.

# Today

Today, we still send letters by mail. Lots and lots of people send e-mails too! Computers make it fast and easy to send e-mails to people who live far away.

# Long Ago

Long ago, many people traveled on horseback. It took a long time to travel from place to place. The horses could not always move very fast. The horses sometimes pulled carts and carriages with people in them.

# Today

Today, cars and buses often get us where we are going quickly. Roads and highways make it easy to travel to other places. New kinds of cars are always being made. These new cars might make travel even easier in years to come!

# Glossary

**community**  a group of people and the place where they live

**electricity**  a form of energy

**neighborhood**  a place where people live, work, and play

# Changing Communities

by Ellen Bari

Editorial Offices: Glenview, Illinois • Parsippany, New Jersey • New York, New York
Sales Offices: Needham, Massachusetts • Duluth, Georgia • Glenview, Illinois
Coppell, Texas • Ontario, California • Mesa, Arizona

# Long Ago

Long ago, many houses in the United States were made of wood. Some houses were smaller than those built today. Heat in a house usually came from a fire in a fireplace.

Over the years **communities** have changed. A community is a group of people. A **neighborhood** is where people live, work, and play.

# Today

Today, wood is still used to build houses. Concrete, bricks, glass, and steel are also used. It takes lots of things to build a house.

Many homes in the United States now have heat, running water, and **electricity**. Electricity is a form of energy.

# Long Ago

Long ago, many people wrote letters by hand using pen and paper. They sent these letters to family and friends who lived far away. It could take a long time for the letters to arrive.

# Today

Today, we still send letters by mail. Lots and lots of people send e-mails too! Computers make it fast and easy to send e-mails to people who live far away.

# Long Ago

Long ago, many people traveled on horseback. It took a long time to travel from place to place. The horses could not always move very fast. The horses sometimes pulled carts and carriages with people in them.

# Today

Today, cars and buses often get us where we are going quickly. Roads and highways make it easy to travel to other places. New kinds of cars are always being made. These new cars might make travel even easier in years to come!

# Glossary

**community** a group of people and the place where they live

**electricity** a form of energy

**neighborhood** a place where people live, work, and play

# Changing Communities

by Ellen Bari

Editorial Offices: Glenview, Illinois • Parsippany, New Jersey • New York, New York
Sales Offices: Needham, Massachusetts • Duluth, Georgia • Glenview, Illinois
Coppell, Texas • Ontario, California • Mesa, Arizona

# Long Ago

Long ago, many houses in the United States were made of wood. Some houses were smaller than those built today. Heat in a house usually came from a fire in a fireplace.

Over the years **communities** have changed. A community is a group of people. A **neighborhood** is where people live, work, and play.

# Today

Today, wood is still used to build houses. Concrete, bricks, glass, and steel are also used. It takes lots of things to build a house.

Many homes in the United States now have heat, running water, and **electricity**. Electricity is a form of energy.

# Long Ago

Long ago, many people wrote letters by hand using pen and paper. They sent these letters to family and friends who lived far away. It could take a long time for the letters to arrive.

# Today

Today, we still send letters by mail. Lots and lots of people send e-mails too! Computers make it fast and easy to send e-mails to people who live far away.

# Long Ago

Long ago, many people traveled on horseback. It took a long time to travel from place to place. The horses could not always move very fast. The horses sometimes pulled carts and carriages with people in them.

# Today

Today, cars and buses often get us where we are going quickly. Roads and highways make it easy to travel to other places. New kinds of cars are always being made. These new cars might make travel even easier in years to come!

# Glossary

**community**  a group of people and the place where they live

**electricity**  a form of energy

**neighborhood**  a place where people live, work, and play

# Changing Communities

by Ellen Bari

Editorial Offices: Glenview, Illinois • Parsippany, New Jersey • New York, New York
Sales Offices: Needham, Massachusetts • Duluth, Georgia • Glenview, Illinois
Coppell, Texas • Ontario, California • Mesa, Arizona

# Long Ago

Long ago, many houses in the United States were made of wood. Some houses were smaller than those built today. Heat in a house usually came from a fire in a fireplace.

Over the years **communities** have changed. A community is a group of people. A **neighborhood** is where people live, work, and play.

# Today

Today, wood is still used to build houses. Concrete, bricks, glass, and steel are also used. It takes lots of things to build a house.

Many homes in the United States now have heat, running water, and **electricity**. Electricity is a form of energy.

# Long Ago

Long ago, many people wrote letters by hand using pen and paper. They sent these letters to family and friends who lived far away. It could take a long time for the letters to arrive.

# Today

Today, we still send letters by mail. Lots and lots of people send e-mails too! Computers make it fast and easy to send e-mails to people who live far away.

# Long Ago

Long ago, many people traveled on horseback. It took a long time to travel from place to place. The horses could not always move very fast. The horses sometimes pulled carts and carriages with people in them.

# Today

Today, cars and buses often get us where we are going quickly. Roads and highways make it easy to travel to other places. New kinds of cars are always being made. These new cars might make travel even easier in years to come!

# Glossary

**community**  a group of people and the place where they live

**electricity**  a form of energy

**neighborhood**  a place where people live, work, and play

# Changing Communities

by Ellen Bari

Editorial Offices: Glenview, Illinois • Parsippany, New Jersey • New York, New York
Sales Offices: Needham, Massachusetts • Duluth, Georgia • Glenview, Illinois
Coppell, Texas • Ontario, California • Mesa, Arizona

# Long Ago

Long ago, many houses in the United States were made of wood. Some houses were smaller than those built today. Heat in a house usually came from a fire in a fireplace.

Over the years **communities** have changed. A community is a group of people. A **neighborhood** is where people live, work, and play.

# Today

Today, wood is still used to build houses. Concrete, bricks, glass, and steel are also used. It takes lots of things to build a house.

Many homes in the United States now have heat, running water, and **electricity**. Electricity is a form of energy.

# Long Ago

Long ago, many people wrote letters by hand using pen and paper. They sent these letters to family and friends who lived far away. It could take a long time for the letters to arrive.

# Today

Today, we still send letters by mail. Lots and lots of people send e-mails too! Computers make it fast and easy to send e-mails to people who live far away.

# Long Ago

Long ago, many people traveled on horseback. It took a long time to travel from place to place. The horses could not always move very fast. The horses sometimes pulled carts and carriages with people in them.

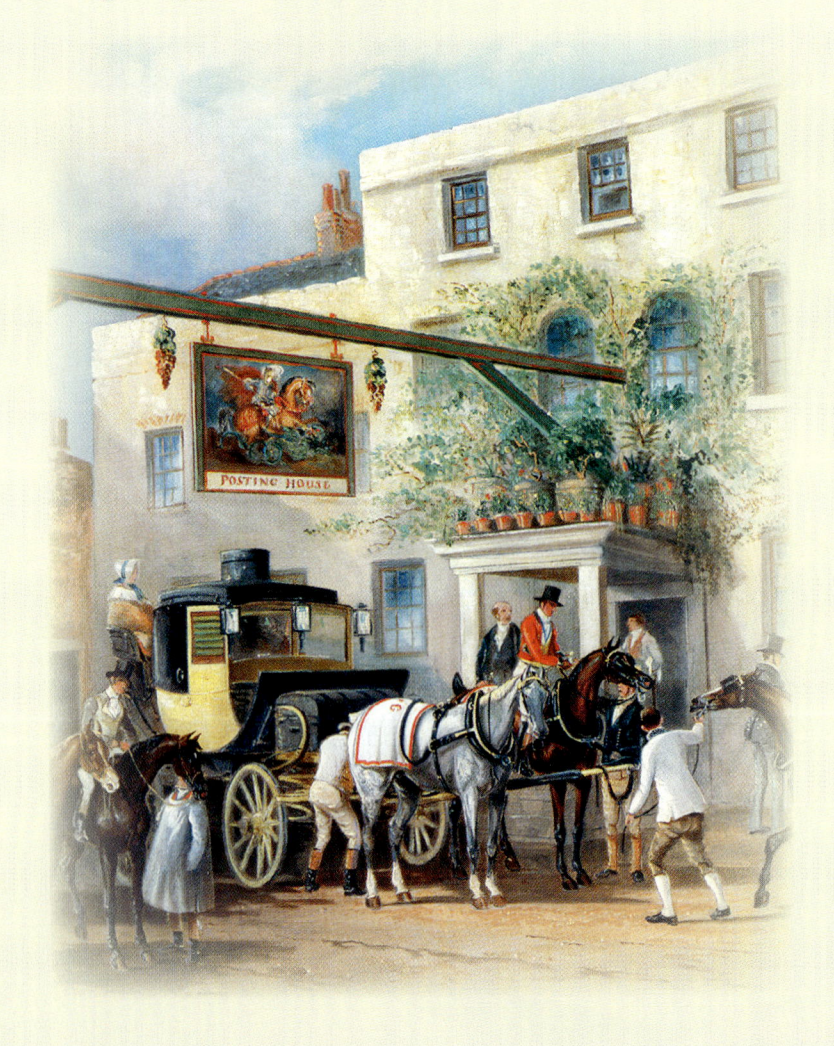

# Today

Today, cars and buses often get us where we are going quickly. Roads and highways make it easy to travel to other places. New kinds of cars are always being made. These new cars might make travel even easier in years to come!

# Glossary

**community** a group of people and the place where they live

**electricity** a form of energy

**neighborhood** a place where people live, work, and play

Social Studies

# Changing Communities

by Ellen Bari

This book is about how communities change over time. It shows how things were long ago and compares them to how they are today.

## Vocabulary
community
neighborhood
electricity

ISBN: 0-328-14794-X

Copyright © Pearson Education, Inc.

All Rights Reserved. Printed in the United States of America. This publication is protected by Copyright, and permission should be obtained from the publisher prior to any prohibited reproduction, storage in a retrieval system, or transmission in any form by any means, electronic, mechanical, photocopying, recording, or likewise. For information regarding permission(s), write to: Permissions Department, Scott Foresman, 1900 East Lake Avenue, Glenview, Illinois 60025.

7 8 9 10  V0G1  14 13 12 11 10 09 08

# Changing Communities

by Ellen Bari

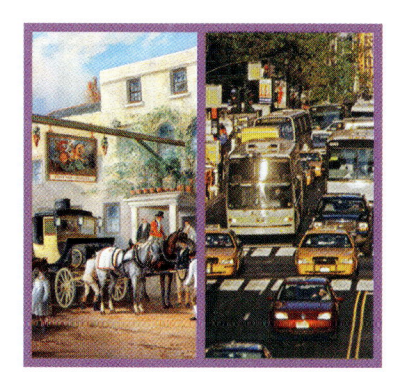

**PEARSON**
Scott Foresman

Editorial Offices: Glenview, Illinois • Parsippany, New Jersey • New York, New York
Sales Offices: Needham, Massachusetts • Duluth, Georgia • Glenview, Illinois
Coppell, Texas • Ontario, California • Mesa, Arizona

# Long Ago

Long ago, many houses in the United States were made of wood. Some houses were smaller than those built today. Heat in a house usually came from a fire in a fireplace.

Over the years **communities** have changed. A community is a group of people. A **neighborhood** is where people live, work, and play.

# Today

Today, wood is still used to build houses. Concrete, bricks, glass, and steel are also used. It takes lots of things to build a house.

Many homes in the United States now have heat, running water, and **electricity**. Electricity is a form of energy.

# Long Ago

Long ago, many people wrote letters by hand using pen and paper. They sent these letters to family and friends who lived far away. It could take a long time for the letters to arrive.

# Today

Today, we still send letters by mail. Lots and lots of people send e-mails too! Computers make it fast and easy to send e-mails to people who live far away.

# Long Ago

Long ago, many people traveled on horseback. It took a long time to travel from place to place. The horses could not always move very fast. The horses sometimes pulled carts and carriages with people in them.

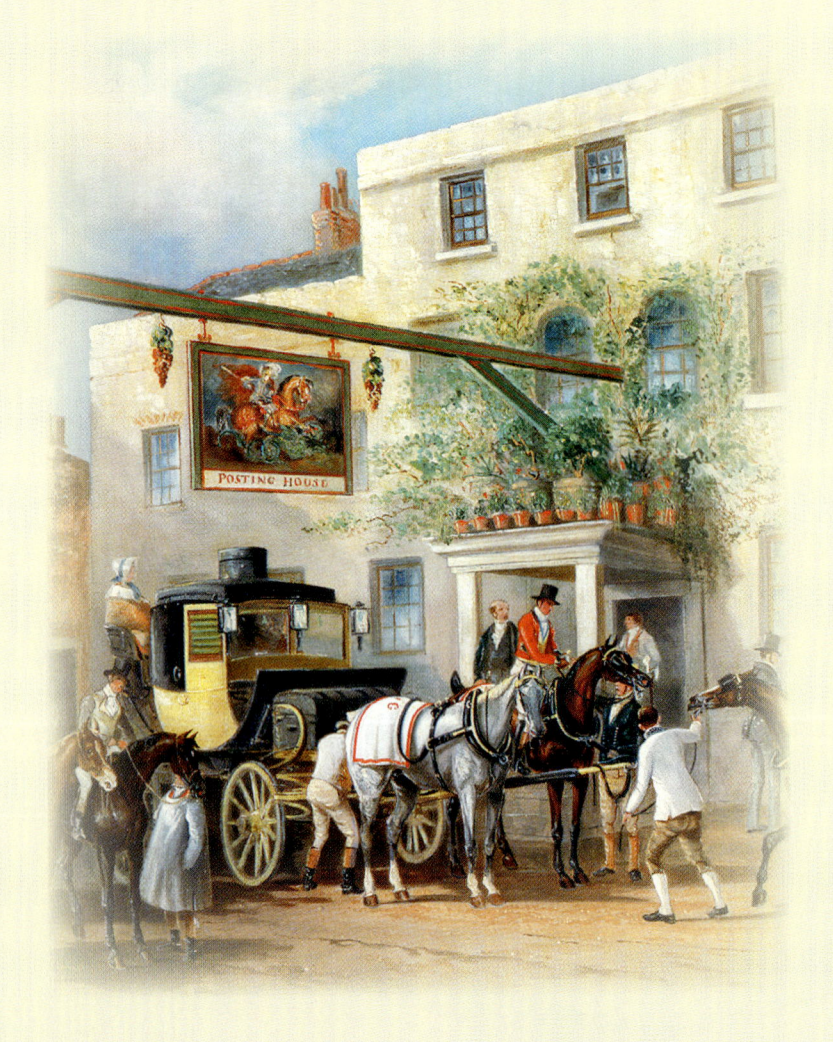

# Today

Today, cars and buses often get us where we are going quickly. Roads and highways make it easy to travel to other places. New kinds of cars are always being made. These new cars might make travel even easier in years to come!

# Glossary

**community** a group of people and the place where they live

**electricity** a form of energy

**neighborhood** a place where people live, work, and play